born to die

jayne gatsby

All rights reserved. No part of this publication may be reproduced, distributed, or transmitted in any form or by any means, including photocopying, recording, or other electronic or mechanical methods, without the prior written permission of the publisher, except in the case of brief quotations embodied in critical reviews and specific other noncommercial uses permitted by copyright law.

i wrapped my heart
  up in this book
  a broken heart
  was all it took

the only person
i'd like to thank
is myself

"born to die"
saved my life

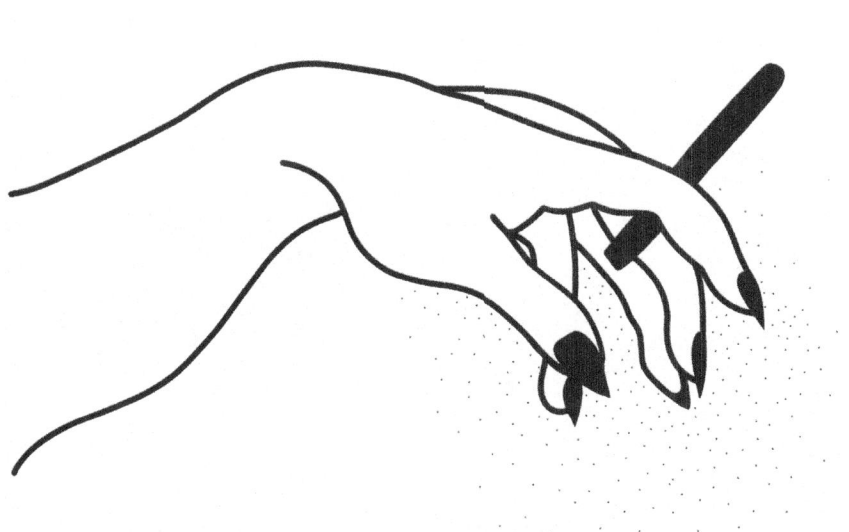

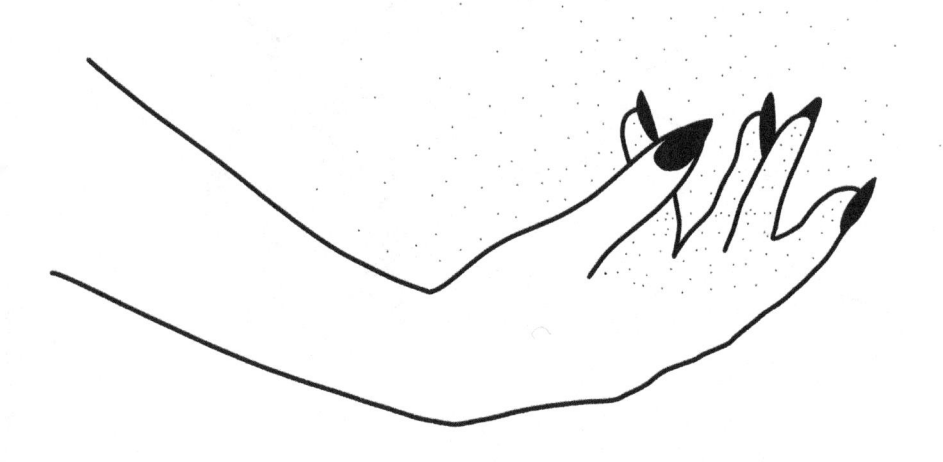

jayne gatsby

in the loving memory of me
this is my eulogy...

a child
once filled with glee
now an adult
full of pain and suffering

i always hoped
i always believed
but disappointment
made my heart grieve

born to die

in my innocence
i died
dead but still alive
i've been mourning
my entire life
disappointment cuts deeper
than a knife

where were you
all my life?

                                                            all i ever wanted
                                                        was for god to care
                                                   begged him to answer
                                                            just one prayer

jayne gatsby

true love
will never die
neither do eras
we keep alive

melancholy melodies
playback
timeless memories

born to die

i think in rhyme
a dark lullaby
poetry cradles us
when we cry

jayne gatsby

poetry is a secret code
that only the broken hearted
understand to know

born to die

grey skies
by the hollywood sign
a place where dreams
come to die

getting high
in high school
was a time
to be alive

jayne gatsby

only the pure of heart
can save the world
don't lose heart
you precious pearl

born to die

vintage music . . .
my mind is sound
reliving a time
with no bound

maybe back then
it could have worked out
born in the wrong era
and i can't get out

jayne gatsby

love feels
like heavenly bliss
betrayal feels
like a burning abyss

life was perfect
as a kid
the closest to heaven
i've ever been

born to die

she was a child
who lost her way
hoping a hero
would save the day

she prayed
for a getaway
shoveling through
heavy memories

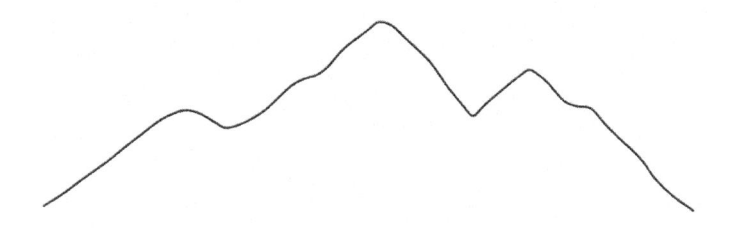

jayne gatsby

i was a princess
stuck in a tower
in my hair
i wore a flower

prayed one day
i'd be saved
by a prince
who never came

i grew up
and no one was here
the dragon i fought
was only my fear

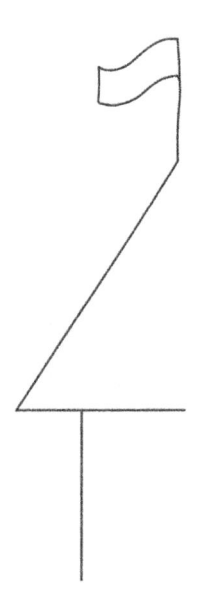

                        i wish fairytales
                             were real
                      a fairy godmother
                      whose always near

born to die

they are doing well
but they refused to treat me well
there is no hope, oh well
even though i wished them well

now i dream by the wishing well
praying that i will get well
my heart is still hurting like hell
wishing for a miracle
by the wishing well

jayne gatsby

questions
have no ending
while the answers
are still pending . . .

born to die

psychology heals
because it reveals
the truth
fear conceals

jayne gatsby

people pleasing
is a response to defeat
a child once aiming
to hold the peace

what is the worst
they can do
that has not already
happened to you?

born to die

anxiety loves to lie
interrupting my life

one
compulsive
thought

at a time

                                      telling me to pray
                                  or someone will die
                                        as if i'm god
                                and can control life

jayne gatsby

there is a soul
that lives in me
who hates the pain
they inflicted on me

born to die

the little me
is the purest thing
that is ever known
in all humanity

she deserved
a happy ending

i guess her prayers
are still sending . . .

jayne gatsby

my inner teen
at war within me
only justice can cure
all her suffering

born to die

the love i had for you
now belongs to me

i guess i am finally
healing

jayne gatsby

i do not want anyone
who knew me
to know me
because they failed
to love me
when they had the chance
they exploited me

love is supposed
to be enough
but to them
it was never
good enough

i guess this is where
this unworthiness
stems from

born to die

the innocent
will always get priority
justice and peace
will be their story

and i would never demand
the glory

jayne gatsby

nightmare by day
justice by night

you cannot run
you cannot hide

i crave justice like
it is my will to life
taking what is wrong
and making it right

born to die

people who preach
are more lost than me
they justify abuse
and have no empathy

where is your accountability?

people who lack personality
lead with their sexuality

born to die

i wish i had
a time machine
to escape this misery

a century
with no greed
with true love
and empathy

my tears are worth more
than the stars in the sky . . .
my inner child
will never die

born to die

everytime i cry
a part of me dies...

you could have done anything
why didn't you try?

jayne gatsby

i wish to live
not just survive
i wish my dreams
would come to life

born to die

nostalgic for a life
i never had
a place where dreams
come to pass

jayne gatsby

why is my innocence
fighting like hell?

                                        where is my justice
                                     to balance the scale?

born to die

i talk to heaven
hoping someone loves me
is that faith
or magical thinking?

jayne gatsby

the pain in my soul
consumes me
i only find comfort
when it's gloomy

born to die

all my summers
were full of pain
but when it was cold
no one ever touched me

jayne gatsby

i find comfort
when the clouds block the sun
the rain cries for me
reminding me of its love

born to die

i feel safe
when it rains
hate the way
the sun shines
on this pain

i wish the rain
washed away the pain
listen and watch
the sky mourning for me

jayne gatsby

time will pass
and so will i
why does it hurt
to be alive?

born to die

heavenly tears
shower me with rain
it pours down
with empathy

jayne gatsby

why is there delay
to the prayers i pray?

born to die

i hate it when you say
"it was always you"
if only i knew
to love me too

abandoned myself
just for you
childhood trauma
made me a fool

jayne gatsby

the way your gaze
made me believe
that no matter what
you would never leave

love cannot
be counterfeit
you cannot
manufacture it

jayne gatsby

purity paints love
with color
sacrificing their love
for another

born to die

love cannot hurt
love cannot betray
it is not found
in love's DNA

jayne gatsby

psychology healed
the wounds in me
after they gaslit
my reality

knowledge saved
my sanity
it could save
humanity

born to die

i will find a way
to save the day
and bring a superhero
to fight your fears away

and to wipe the tears
from your eyes
that you never deserved
to cry

no more scars
on your back
do not worry
they won't come back

you survived
you little star
go shine bright
you'll make it far

jayne gatsby

it is insane
how the same people
who cheered you on
are the same people
waiting on your downfall

born to die

all i wanted
was for you to love me
but instead
you loved to judge me

jayne gatsby

they are loyal
to evil itself
as they betray
everyone else

born to die

i told myself lies
for the sake
of a peaceful mind

only to find
my worst fears
came to life

all i ask is why?
i need peace
in my life

jayne gatsby

time flies
when you're having fun
but time freezes
when you're in love

born to die

driving on the hill
holding hands as the
warm rain poured
on the windshield

we danced in the rain
as the palm trees swayed
we kissed all day
catching sun rays

i miss that
two story house
where love was born
where love was found

jayne gatsby

dirty dancing in the pool
that island love
made me a fool

shooting stars in our sight
jacuzzi bubbles
in the moonlight

resorts and hotels
we snuck in both
you said you loved me
like an oath

i miss the smell
of the ocean breeze
the sound of waves
forever crashing

these beautiful memories
riddle me with pain
did it hurt you
the way it hurt me?

born to die

like two kids
we ran through the door
on the balcony
we kissed some more

laughing all
our cares away
i miss the days
we used to pray

i'll never forget
the smell of the rain
i begged god
to help you stay

dreaming of what
life could be

jayne gatsby

felt like heaven
when you're around
got me missing
that two story house

born to die

i never want
to see you again
you sold me a dream
i could never forget

jayne gatsby

i wish you never
existed
never met a human
more twisted

born to die

the scars remind me
of what once was there
i cry because
i wish you cared

jayne gatsby

there is no way life
could be this unfair
the price i paid
for ignorance

born to die

who knew revenge
could be so sweet
only returning back
what you brought
to me

jayne gatsby

those
with bad intentions
are always looking
for more attention

born to die

the lights flickered
in my eyes
like a vintage film
restored to life

in my world
it's black and white
the way the moon
shines bright at night

jayne gatsby

did you feel my pain?
but did it hurt you less
than it hurt me?

born to die

your love became venom
burning in my veins
i made the mistake
talking to a snake

jayne gatsby

everytime i walk
down memory lane
i run into you
and it hurts the same

i turned this pain
into poetry
i turned brokenness
into beauty

born to die

when we sing
about pain
it makes us feel
less lonely

jayne gatsby

you were a warning sign

that i didn't love myself
enough to try

the only good i wish
is goodbye

born to die

i wasn't created
to sit around
'til you decide
to figure it out

jayne gatsby

i write poetry
when i'm in pain
i lack joy
in everything

the world is not ending
doom is not always
impending
energy wasted in lies and fears
they never deserved
my tears

born to die

i fell in love
with our memories
fantasizing about
a happier ending

instead i fell
into hell
only truth
can break the spell

jayne gatsby

i do not know
what happiness is
i thought it was you
but you were counterfeit

happiness my home
was a person
hope is one
of the worst delusions

just need something
heavenly and right
the way love was
before the beginning of time

when the audience's
favorite characters
fall in love . . .

do you remember
when those characters
were us?

jayne gatsby

all i wanted
was your heart to shine
why'd you go
and have to break mine?

born to die

there was no love in you
but what i loved
was my reflection in you

jayne gatsby

the scars of betrayal
never healed
because of these wounds
i hate how i feel

unsafe
and unreal
out of touch
ethereal

born to die

no one can steal
my soul's delight
i see my childhood
as a golden light
it shines so lovely
it shines so bright
i saw it once
in a dream at night

jayne gatsby

i wish i had peace
when i sleep
my dreams relive
painful memories
i wish for love
i wish for peace
all i want is a
happily ever ending

born to die

stop babbling your
delusions at me while
justifying your insanity
your hypocritical mouth
infuriates me
rotting in your codependency

all you do is suck my energy
a demon in a human body

jayne gatsby

your love is like candy
sweet but so unhealthy

born to die

my imagination
saved my life

maybe it existed
in another life

jayne gatsby

psychology set me free
it ripped the lies
right out of me

i finally see reality
and not through the lens
of their gaslighting

born to die

i was a child
looking for heaven
church destroyed my life
at eleven

jayne gatsby

i want to be alone
in a world i call home

a place where dreams
never die
where the pure of heart
only thrive

born to die

anyone who looked at me
with evil in their eyes
i hope hell
keeps you warm at night

jayne gatsby

my own mind
surprises me
a place that tries
to comfort me
my mind is always
there for me
my mind is where
love can dream

born to die

all i ever wanted
was unconditional love
i created a world
with every puff

jayne gatsby

i won't give up
not this time
i will heal
even if
it takes a lifetime

born to die

never forget the truth
never go back
to the abuse

there will never be
another you

jayne gatsby

loving me
is like magic
sparks fly
feeling electric

born to die

i know heaven exists
because my heart
yearns for it

jayne gatsby

if you loved yourself right
you could have had me
in another life

born to die

look at the hell
i've been through
all because i thought
you were good

jayne gatsby

one of a kind
kind of dime
the kind of love
that makes you rhyme

born to die

the kind of love
that freezes time
the type of love
that's always kind

jayne gatsby

i miss when love
was never sad
i miss the childhood
i never had

born to die

i cried so many
unnecessary tears
all because
you weren't here

jayne gatsby

they think i am working
with a team
but that is just my multiple
personalities

born to die

i got high
off your demise
watch the truth
eat you alive

jayne gatsby

ask and you shall receive
but i almost died
asking and believing

i begged and cried
for years and years
does my plea
not matter here?

born to die

the imagination
you see on tv
is what we imagine
love to be

perfectly directed by
the mind of my dream
i wish love became
reality

jayne gatsby

nightmares
haunt me at night
reminding me of the pain
i feel inside

born to die

religion convinced me that
life begins when you die
but why can't i live
while i'm still alive?

jayne gatsby

i wish i had love
that i didn't need to
search for
mourn for
or not be "good enough" for

born to die

religion said
my pain is nothing more
than a pawn in life's game

they condemned me for using
my logical brain
what more did i expect
from the clinically insane?

my whole life became
a guessing game
lost and confused
in their cruel faith

i prayed
through the pain
how am i still
the one to blame?

jayne gatsby

just because evil exists
does not mean i need
to participate in it

born to die

i've been burned
i've been dropped
begged back
with the baggage of mistrust

i remember the lies
i remember the pain
i wish to escape
all the bad memories

jayne gatsby

i knew
hell was real
by the evil
you felt comfortable in

born to die

i play dirty
like the villains did
before me
a princess who never got
a happy story
even your smear campaigns
can't destory me

jayne gatsby

you hate the way
i beat your game
you thought you won
but checkmate

born to die

i am a princess
who saved herself
i am here
and no one else

jayne gatsby

you loved me
out of spite
pretending to be
my shining knight
exploited my pain
for your delight

i wish i was
not polite
and caught
the next flight

people never get better
with time

born to die

my eyes go blurry
when i dissociate
in disbelief
of my fate

test the real
from the fake
expose the truth
for justice sake

jayne gatsby

did i mention
how much i hate this dimension
searching for love
while they search for attention

did i mention
the pain and depression
of a heavenly soul
with no bad intentions

born to die

it is evil
to bless someone
who is evil

jayne gatsby

our love felt
like twilight
dancing in
the moonlight
shooting stars
shine so bright
electric love
is our ignite
i wish i may
i wish i might
to live my dream
my dream tonight

born to die

when i get high
i believe in god
who created the sky

then i repent
and start to cry
even in innocence
i feel guilty inside

i feel like a child
who deserved a better life
please allow me
to enter your heavenly skies
as long as i exist
please
don't ever leave my side

i enter the pearly gates
to be by your side

religious trauma has ruined my life

jayne gatsby

the way you made me feel
sealed the deal
pain was the only closure
i needed to heal

born to die

i checked the boxes
off my bucket list
yet there is still
a feeling of emptiness

jayne gatsby

i love the girl
i used to be
she was kind
when they were mean

"if only you just believe"
then i went to therapy

born to die

if i loved myself
as much as i love them
life could be heaven

jayne gatsby

i'd rather feel the pain
of clarity
than to deny reality

born to die

a champion
who fought the fight
her gold medal
shined so bright

crowned a hero
wearing gold
diamonds shine
icy cold

jayne gatsby

i believe
our love for each other
will help us live
so much longer

born to die

life has no meaning
it is only meant for healing

jayne gatsby

i love it when the moon
shines over me
through the window blinds
it sees me
it shines so bright
upon me
i lay on my side
and watch it gleam

i love how the moon
always finds me

born to die

if i genuinely could
i genuinely would

jayne gatsby

i wish we could live forever
and relive the eras
we've been together

born to die

it was real
but it felt surreal

jayne gatsby

why am i mourning
the days i've been alive?
could i redo it perfectly
in another life?

is that what heaven is?
a place with no goodbyes
a place where love lives

born to die

you went crazy
trying to understand
but they went crazy
when you found out

jayne gatsby

hours feel like minutes
minutes feel like hours

born to die

i only give empathy
to those who give empathy

jayne gatsby

there was a part of me
that died
when you were no longer
in my life

born to die

i told so many people
about the abuse
not one of them cared
although they knew

jayne gatsby

my heart burns
for another try
but only in
another life

in a different dimension
in a different time
where you never committed
those crimes

born to die

why'd you go
and be the bad guy?

was it so hard
to simply try?

maybe you were different
in another life

jayne gatsby

i held the light
with all my might
you are dead while
you are still alive

maybe we were different
in another life

born to die

i mourn your death
while you're alive
forever is still
not enough time

jayne gatsby

discover yourself
be you and no one else

you live
then you die
so enjoy life

never comfort yourself
with lies
or else the truth
will be your demise

born to die

and on tv
i escape reality
just to live
another life
vicariously

jayne gatsby

my gut showed me
before i could see
that i was right
about everything

this pain has
validity
this pain
never lied to me

born to die

i tried for years
to understand your abuse
and why you do
what you do

jayne gatsby

i think about you
from time to time
music sounds different
when i'm high

born to die

we live in a world
where beauty is a threat
and they feel validated
hurting the innocent
to hate someone
without regret

i hate this world
we're living in . . .

jayne gatsby

blissfully
oblivious

born to die

hell gained another demon

jayne gatsby

heaven gained another angel

born to die

if the truth
is the truth
then let the truth do
what it needs to do

jayne gatsby

if why + how = who
then you always knew

born to die

pain is temporary
when inflicted externally
but emotional pain
seems to last for eternity

jayne gatsby

statue of david
by my bedside
writing sad poems
is a way to confide
in myself
and in the hope
of a divine

born to die

i've met atheists
more moral than you
empathy is our access
to the truth

we protect the abused
something you
and your god
never do

jayne gatsby

if you fall in love
with a lie
it takes pain
to break the tie

don't you worry
don't you cry
the truth will shine
the brightest light

born to die

avoiding evil
is the way
we survive
in a world
built on lies

only the guilty
never apologize

jayne gatsby

sin is abuse
abuse is sin

is that not clear enough
to religious bigots?

born to die

you cannot reason
with insanity
all it does is
create calamity

jayne gatsby

i was okay
with not being okay
and it was beautiful
in a dreamy way

born to die

fame makes you pay
with your privacy
for a little more
pocket change

… jayne gatsby

they preach
to convince themselves
a belief
because they lack
authenticity

born to die

i can't believe
these are the people
i never got to choose
who knew life
could be so cruel
they live to abuse
stop trying to fix
their loose screws

jayne gatsby

i just need
arms to hold
me
with someone
whose never cold
towards me
who never ceases
to love me
who will always act
justly

with a mind
that is trusting
with a heart
never judging

born to die

thank you
for proving me
right

you disappointed me
right on time

jayne gatsby

i am tired of feeling guilty
for them taking accountability

born to die

poetry
is the purest form of pain
pain writes itself
so effortlessly

jayne gatsby

i am stardust
yearning for a heavenly place
i love how the planets
twinkle from space

born to die

parents who villainize children
never deserved them

jayne gatsby

i am not searching
for notoriety
i would rather speak
through my writing

born to die

spirit of truth
forgive me of my sins
forgive me of my ignorance

jayne gatsby

i hope karma
eats you alive
i can't wait to see
the truth come to light

born to die

save those feelings
for yourself
you deserve them more
than anyone else

jayne gatsby

when too much
of a bad thing happens to you
it changes you
and the pain still hurts
as it used to

born to die

i cried your death
a thousand times
you were dead
while you were still alive
without an ounce of love inside
you found peace when i cried
human beings with demons inside
they never change
they always lie
they never change
even when they die

jayne gatsby

i am only genuinely happy
for genuine people
because they hate
every form of evil
no selfish bone
in their body
they show love
to everybody

born to die

so many years
so many tears

jayne gatsby

stop trying to be me
it is fucking creepy

born to die

you solidified
by proving me right
disappointment arrived
right on time

sometimes i hate
always being right

jayne gatsby

i do not want you
lurking from a distance
in fact
better yet
forget my existence

born to die

patterns never lie
proven right
many times

jayne gatsby

narcissism
is the root to all evil

born to die

my heart hurts for a childhood i missed
somehow my heart still hurts for it
my nervous system remembers a story
opposite of the lies that were told to me

jayne gatsby

grow up
without growing cold
we will bloom
as we get old

age means you are alive
only a demon shames
your existence of life

born to die

i wanted to hurt you
as bad as you hurt me
taste my pain
and my suffering

do you like it
when i match your energy?
you awakened the villain
within me

i woke up
and chose violence
i crave justice
for breakfast

if the truth
is your kryptonite
then i won
every fight

you can run
but cannot hide
this story ends
the way i like

jayne gatsby

even when i didn't have a dime
to my name
they loved to guilt me
like a slave

i have no hope
for humanity
because of their lack
of empathy

born to die

perfect in pink
princess canopy
watching tv shows
on the hello kitty tv
shared so many
happy memories
bubbles in the air
bliss without a care

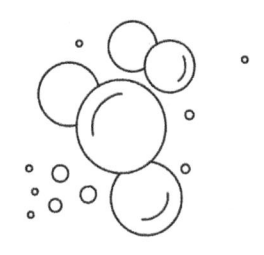

jayne gatsby

she was my age
she was my angel
she protected me
from that evil
she hid me away
for freedom sake
the peace was so boring
i miss it in every way

born to die

people forget that delusion
is believable too
who thought
who knew

jayne gatsby

smart people
don't need you
to overexplain
their aim is to understand
without judging

born to die

the only reason
you're confused
is because you keep
denying the truth

jayne gatsby

i was in love
with the idea of you
crazy how an idea
can destroy you

born to die

so little time
wish those parents
were mine
i dream about it
when i'm high
i play pretend
in my mind

jayne gatsby

i don't wanna die
no need to say goodbye
my peace is more important
than these trauma ties

good riddance
and goodbye
i choose to live
my life

born to die

in another life
i'm a poet
who knew pain
but never showed it
thought poetically
and beautifully wrote it

i deserve the love
i give everyone else
the best i can do
is be myself

i was born to live
not born to die
to live in truth
free from the lies

Complete the Cover Art Collection

Exclusively Available on Amazon

Made in the USA
Coppell, TX
01 September 2023